D0811756

HEINEMANN
STATE STUDIES

All Around
New York

Mark Stewart

Grinnell Library
2642 East Main St.
Wappingers Falls, NY 12590
845-297-3428

Heinemann Library
Chicago, Illinois

© 2003 Heinemann Library
a division of Reed Elsevier Inc.
Chicago, IL

Customer Service 888-454-2279

Visit our website at www.heinemannlibrary.com

All rights reserved. No part of this publication may
be reproduced or transmitted in any form or by
any means, electronic or mechanical, including
photocopying, recording, taping, or any
nformation storage and retrieval system, without
permission in writing from the publisher.

Designed by Heinemann Library
Printed and bound by Lake Book Manufacturing

07 06 05 04 03
10 9 8 7 6 5 4 3 2 1

**Library of Congress Cataloging-in-
Publication Data**
Stewart, Mark.
  All around New York : regions and resources :
New York State studies /
Mark Stewart.
      v. cm.
Summary: Provides a look at New York's different
geographical regions and the industry and econo-
my of each. Includes bibliographical references
(p.) and index.
Contents: An introduction to New York -- New
York City and metropolitan area -- Long Island --
The Hudson Valley -- The Catskills -- The
Capital-Saratoga area -- The Central-Leatherstock-
ing region -- Northern New York -- The Finger
Lakes -- Western New York.
    ISBN 1-4034-0352-X -- ISBN 1-4034-0574-3
(pbk.)
1. New York (State)--Geography--Juvenile literature. 2.Regionalism--New York (State)--Juvenile literature. [1. New York (State)--Geography.] I. Title.
    F119.3.S747 2003
    974.7--dc21

2002154318

Acknowledgments
The author and publishers are grateful to the
following for permission to reproduce copyright
material:

Cover photographs by (top, L-R) Rudi Von
Briel/Heinemann Library, Rudi Von Briel/
Heinemann Library, Gail Mooney/Corbis, Rudi
Von Briel/Heinemann Library; (main) Dave G.
Hauser/Corbis

Title page (L-R) Bettmann/Corbis, David
Muench/Corbis, Gail Mooney/Corbis; contents
page, p. 21 NYS Thruway Authority; p. 4 Robert
Lifson/Heinemann Library; pp. 5, 7, 8, 9, 12, 45
maps.com/Heinemann Library; p. 10 Reuters
NewMedia Inc./Corbis; p. 11 Paul Almasy/Corbis;
p. 13T Gail Mooney/Corbis; p. 13B Kevin Fleming/
Corbis; p. 15 Kit Kittle/Corbis; pp. 16, 35 George
Ostertag; p. 17 Stuart Ramson/AP Wide World
Photos; pp. 18, 24, 33 Scott Braut; p. 19T Roger
Ressmeyer/Corbis; p. 19B Bettmann/Corbis; pp.
20, 32, 39, 44 David Muench/Corbis; pp. 22, 23T,
26, 30, 34 Rudi Von Briel/Heinemann Library;
p. 23B Charles E. Rotkin/Corbis; p. 25 Francis X.
Driscoll; p. 27 Lee Snider/Corbis; p. 28 Ruth Smiley/
Mohonk Mountain House/AP Wide World Photos;
p. 29 David A. Brownell; p. 37 Roman Soumar/
Corbis; pp. 38T, 42 H. Armstrong Roberts; p. 38B
Lee Snider/Corbis; p. 40 Doug Wilson/Corbis;
p. 41 David Ruether Photography

Photo research by Kathy Creech

Special thanks to expert reader Edward H.
Knoblauch. Knoblauch has an MA from Syracuse
University in American History, is the webmaster
for New York History Net (www.nyhistory.com),
and was the managing editor of the Encyclopedia
of New York State.

Every effort has been made to contact copyright
holders of any material reproduced in this book.
Any omissions will be rectified in subsequent
printings if notice is given to the publisher.

Some words are shown in bold, **like this.**
You can find out what they mean by looking
in the glossary.

Contents

An Introduction to New York

When people think of New York state, they might picture New York City or the Statue of Liberty. Maybe they would think of towering Niagara Falls, or the city of Buffalo buried deep in snow. All of these thoughts would be correct. New York is an amazingly **varied** state. It has ocean beaches and rugged peaks. It has dairy farms and skyscrapers. From its **natural resources** to its many businesses, and from its **climate** to its cities, New York is one of the most **diverse** places in the United States.

This book covers nine geographic areas in New York: the New York City and Metropolitan area, Long Island, the Hudson Valley, the Catskills, the Capital-Saratoga region, the Central-Leatherstocking region, Northern New York, the Finger Lakes, and Western New York.

• •

Times Square is one of the most visited areas of New York City. It attracts around 30 million visitors each year.

New York Regions

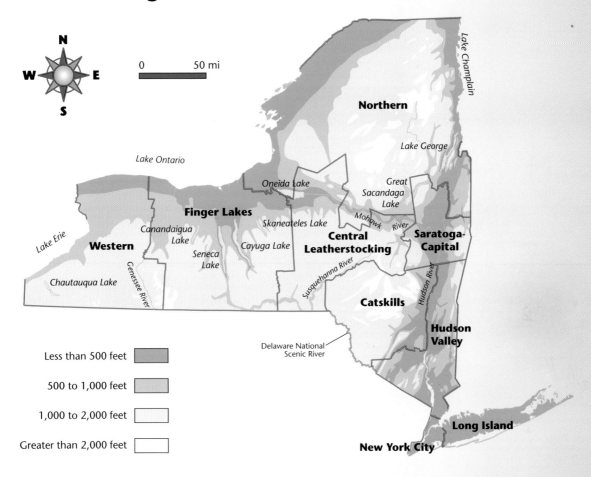

Northern

Lake Champlain

Lake George

Lake Ontario

Oneida Lake

Great Sacandaga Lake

Finger Lakes

Skaneateles Lake

Mohawk River

Saratoga-Capital

Canandaigua Lake

Lake Erie

Western

Seneca Lake

Cayuga Lake

Central Leatherstocking

Susquehanna River

Hudson River

Genessee River

Chautauqua Lake

Catskills

Delaware National Scenic River

Hudson Valley

Long Island

New York City

Less than 500 feet	
500 to 1,000 feet	
1,000 to 2,000 feet	
Greater than 2,000 feet	

*The nine geographic regions of New York each have a range of **landforms** and **topography**.*

New York is located in the northeastern United States. To the north, it is bordered by the Canadian province Quebec and one of the Great Lakes, Lake Ontario. Another of the Great Lakes, Lake Erie, borders New York to the west. The states Pennsylvania and New Jersey border New York to the south. To the east are Vermont, Massachusetts, and Connecticut.

Depending on where you are in the state, New York's climate and precipitation vary greatly. Rainfall varies from 35 to 60 inches per year. Temperatures can also be very different. Near the Atlantic Ocean on the southeast coast of the state, temperatures are more mild than in other parts of New York. This means that in the winter, New York City, which is near the ocean, will probably have rain while Buffalo, in the northern part of the state, will have snow.

To find out more about New York's climate, see the map on page 8.

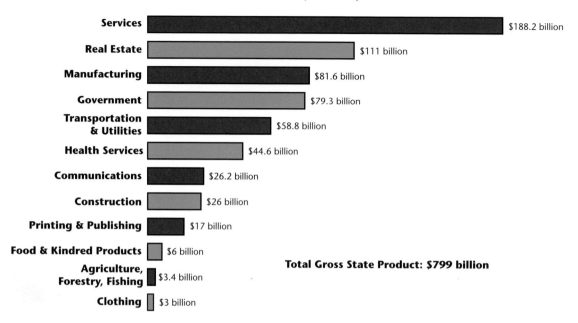

The New York Economy
Its Natural, Capital, and Human Resources
Gross State Product (in dollars)

Services	$188.2 billion
Real Estate	$111 billion
Manufacturing	$81.6 billion
Government	$79.3 billion
Transportation & Utilities	$58.8 billion
Health Services	$44.6 billion
Communications	$26.2 billion
Construction	$26 billion
Printing & Publishing	$17 billion
Food & Kindred Products	$6 billion
Agriculture, Forestry, Fishing	$3.4 billion
Clothing	$3 billion

Total Gross State Product: $799 billion

New York has a wide range of products and services that bring money into the state.

MANUFACTURING

If New York were a country, it would rank as having the ninth largest economy in the world. Its **gross state product** is nearly $800 billion a year. This is the result of all products that are produced in the state of New York each year. New York is home to headquarters for 55 major companies, including IBM, Fisher Price/Mattel, Kraft Foods, and Eastman Kodak.

Those who are familiar only with New York City might be surprised to learn that New York is a major **agricultural** producer. In fact, one-quarter of the state's land is used by almost 40,000 farmers to produce all kinds of fruits, flowers, vegetables, and livestock. More than half of all agricultural production in New York revolves around dairy products. New York ranks third nationwide in dairy production.

NATURAL RESOURCES

In New York's 54,475 square miles, there are many **natural resources.** For example, New York's 7,251 square miles of lakes and rivers, along with its location on the Atlantic coast, provide a huge supply of seafood

New York Resources

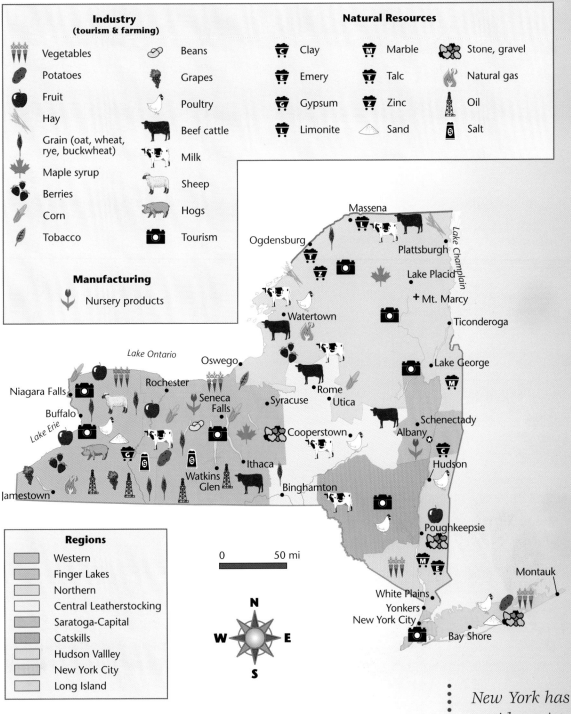

Industry
(tourism & farming)

- Vegetables
- Potatoes
- Fruit
- Hay
- Grain (oat, wheat, rye, buckwheat)
- Maple syrup
- Berries
- Corn
- Tobacco

- Beans
- Grapes
- Poultry
- Beef cattle
- Milk
- Sheep
- Hogs
- Tourism

Natural Resources

- C Clay
- E Emery
- G Gypsum
- L Limonite
- M Marble
- T Talc
- Z Zinc
- Sand
- Stone, gravel
- Natural gas
- Oil
- S Salt

Manufacturing

- Nursery products

Regions

- Western
- Finger Lakes
- Northern
- Central Leatherstocking
- Saratoga-Capital
- Catskills
- Hudson Vallley
- New York City
- Long Island

0   50 mi

N W E S

Map labels: Massena, Ogdensburg, Plattsburgh, Lake Champlain, Lake Placid, Mt. Marcy, Ticonderoga, Watertown, Lake George, Lake Ontario, Oswego, Rochester, Seneca Falls, Rome, Utica, Syracuse, Niagara Falls, Buffalo, Lake Erie, Cooperstown, Schenectady, Albany, Hudson, Ithaca, Watkins Glen, Binghamton, Jamestown, Poughkeepsie, White Plains, Yonkers, New York City, Bay Shore, Montauk

and freshwater fish. Water resources also help to draw visitors to New York each year.

New York's mountains are another natural resource. They are useful because the snowfall that melts off them provides fresh water, and their beauty draws

New York has a wide variety of important resources across all its regions.

New York Precipitation

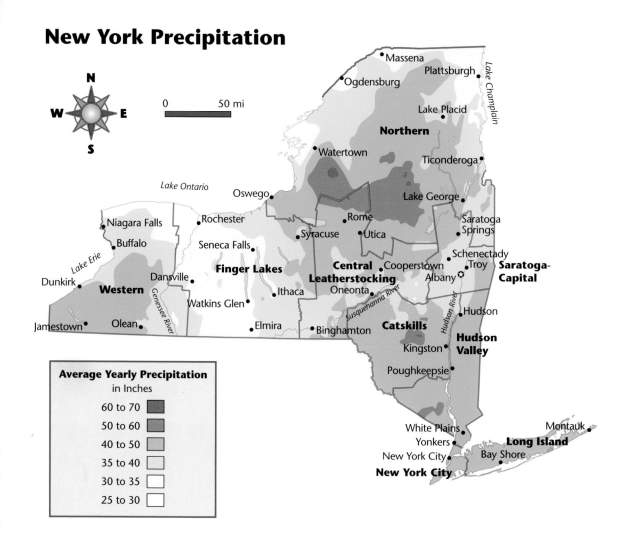

Average Yearly Precipitation
in Inches

60 to 70	
50 to 60	
40 to 50	
35 to 40	
30 to 35	
25 to 30	

Precipitation is the water that falls to the earth. In New York, the amount of precipitation varies greatly around the state.

visitors from across the state and around the world. New York's highest point is in the Adirondack Mountains, at Mount Marcy. Mount Marcy's peak is 5,344 feet above sea level—that's over a mile high!

TOURISM AND TRAVEL

Attractions such as the Adirondack Mountains, Niagara Falls, the Statue of Liberty, and Long Island beaches bring many visitors to New York each year. New York is the third most visited state, after California and Florida. New York's **diverse** population is another of its great resources. Perhaps that is why New York is a favorite destination for people visiting from other countries.

To help people get around, New York offers almost every kind of transportation. New York is 330 miles long

New York Transportation

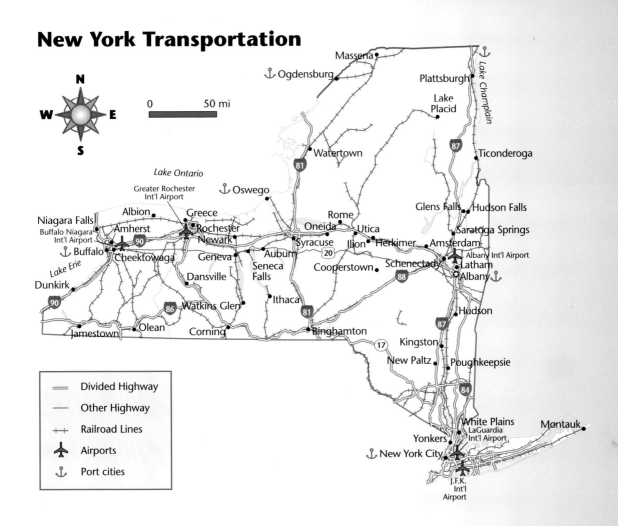

and 283 miles wide. It has an extensive system of rivers, **canals,** highways, airports, and trains that make it a popular place for travel and trade for the entire country. Because of New York's geography, **climate,** and transportation systems, people in the state have many choices about where to live, visit, and work.

Over nineteen million people live and work all around New York's nine regions. One in ten works in manufacturing. These people make things you can touch with your hands, such as coats, candles, or cars. About one in six New Yorkers has a job in government. One in five work in a trade—they might be a mechanic, a veterinarian, or a house painter. No matter what people do for work in New York, there are all kinds of opportunities in each of its regions.

Transportation routes such as highways, rivers, and railroads have made New York the state that it is today.

New York City and Metropolitan Area

New York City's more than eight million residents live in five **boroughs:** Manhattan, Brooklyn, Queens, the Bronx, and Staten Island. New York City has more people than any other city in the United States. Only eight states in the U.S. have a larger population than the population of New York City.

Europeans established New Amsterdam, the first European settlement in New York, on Manhattan Island in the 1600s. Since then, New York City has been a destination for **immigrants** from all over the world. The Statue of Liberty was completed in New York **Harbor** in 1886. It stands as a symbol for the millions of people who have come to America in search of a new life.

To find out more about New York's regions, see the map on page 5.

The New York Stock Exchange, Federal Hall, and the Federal Reserve Bank help make the skyline of lower Manhattan, which is at the heart of the world financial market.

SERVICES

Many people who immigrated to the United States stayed in New York City's five boroughs, and people are the region's biggest resource today. They create a **diverse** population that gives the city a **culture** like none other. These people have different skills, languages, traditions, and ways of life.

The result is a city rich in the arts, communications, finance, and entertainment. There are 20,000 places to eat, 20,000 places to shop, 500 museums and galleries, 250 theaters, and 100 colleges and universities. New York City draws more than 30 million visitors a year.

*New York's most visited park, Central Park, is in uptown Manhattan. It has two skating rinks, a zoo, a castle, a merry-go-round, an open-air theater, a boating lake, and a huge **reservoir.***

The places tourists and residents visit employ workers. Most of these workers are in what is called the service **industry.** They work in hotels, in health care facilities, and other places that provide other services to people and businesses. Service industries account for the largest portion of New York's **gross state product.**

FINANCE

New York City is home to many banks and large financial companies. More money flows through lower Manhattan than anywhere else on Earth. The banks that are based in New York City help finance businesses all over the United States and around the world. The New York Stock Exchange and American Stock Exchange are based in New York City. Many **real estate** and insurance firms are also headquartered in New York City.

To find out more about New York's gross state product, see the graph on page 6.

Five Boroughs of New York City

*Except for the Bronx, New York City's five **boroughs** are all located on islands.*

THE ARTS

The arts include things related to the theater, museums, and performances. The arts employ over 130,000 people in New York City. They generate over $11 billion in **revenue** for the area.

Famous theaters on Broadway are in midtown Manhattan. On the Upper West Side of Manhattan are the Lincoln Center for the Performing Arts, the American Museum of Natural History, and Hayden Planetarium. The Metropolitan Museum of Art, the Whitney Museum of American Art, and the Solomon R. Guggenheim Museum are on the Upper East Side.

MANUFACTURING AND INDUSTRY

New York City is among the leading manufacturing centers in the U.S. It has about 17,000 **industrial** plants that employ over 430,000 workers. The most important industries there are publishing and clothing production.

The Brooklyn Bridge, which links the boroughs of Brooklyn and Manhattan, has six lanes of traffic and carries around 145,000 vehicles each day.

The midtown section of Manhattan, where most New Yorkers go to work each day, is where many of the books and magazines you read and much of the advertising you see is created. New York City has more printing plants than any other city in the United States. It creates one-third of all the books published in the U.S. Many media groups have headquarters in New York City, including the three major television networks.

Over 100,000 people in New York City work in the clothing industry. There are factories for all kinds of other products, too, such as paper products, food products, and machinery. These goods are sold through the **wholesale** trade. New York City has the biggest wholesale grocery and dry-goods companies in the U.S. Other goods are sold at department stores and specialty shops, or retailers. They carry all kinds of products, not just those produced in New York City.

Structures from two World's Fairs (1939–1940 and 1964–1965) stand at Flushing Meadows Park in Queens. Both fairs were held on the site, once a city dump.

Building and construction are **industries** that have made New York City into what it is today. Many recognizable buildings and structures add to the city's appeal and help attract visitors. The Empire State Building, the Chrysler Building, Trinity Church, the Brooklyn Bridge, St. Patrick's Cathedral, and Grand Central Station are some popular sites to visit.

Some industries that greatly contributed to New York City's past have changed over the years. For many years, the **borough** of Brooklyn was known for Brooklyn Navy Yards, where countless ships were built and repaired between the Civil War and World War II. The Navy Yards have been shut down for many years, but part

Getting Around

In a city the size of New York, getting around can be a big challenge. In the 1800s, the city built elevated railroad lines above the streets and created horse-drawn trolley lines. To get on and off the island of Manhattan, you had to take a ferry, a type of boat that transports people.

Trolleys and elevated trains were replaced by **subways** starting in 1904. By the 1930s, this system handled up to two million riders a day. Today, it is over 800 miles long! With the arrival of the automobile, horse-drawn carriages gave way to taxis, and buses replaced trolleys. Major highways were built on the east and west sides of Manhattan, as well as in the other boroughs.

Moving between boroughs also got simpler. Starting with the Brooklyn Bridge in 1882, New York City began building bridges and tunnels to handle the ever-increasing amount of traffic in the area. Today, major bridges in the region include the George Washington, Queensborough, Manhattan, Verrazano Narrows, Williamsburgh, Throgs Neck, Whitestone, and Tri-Borough. The Lincoln, Midtown, Brooklyn Battery, and Holland tunnels also serve the city.

of the area has been made into an industrial park for factories, shipbuilding, and warehouses. More recently, filmmakers have started using the large buildings.

TRANSPORTATION

Rail transportation transformed New York City and makes it able to operate to this day. Once rail lines were in place, people who worked on the island of Manhattan could live in the surrounding boroughs. Queens was a quiet farming community until the Long Island Rail Road added a northern line in 1910. Thousands of city residents moved from cramped apartments to small homes. They **commuted** to their offices. Queens today is a major transportation **hub.** It is home to New York City's two major airports: La Guardia and John F. Kennedy.

The Bronx, the only part of New York City attached to the **mainland,** was also a farming community until an elevated railroad line was built. Tens of thousands of new **immigrants** came there for the wide open spaces, and by the early 1900s, the population skyrocketed to nearly 250,000 people. Today, there are over one million.

The **Port** of New York and New Jersey, in New York City, is an important shipping center. It is one of the world's busiest seaports. Around 200,000 people work there. One in every 10 items that comes into the U.S. enters through this New York City port.

We're Surrounded!

Few people realize that the majority of New York City residents live, work, and play on islands. The Bronx is the only borough that is not completely surrounded by water. Manhattan and Staten Island are both islands, and Queens and Brooklyn make up the western tip of Long Island. There are more than a dozen other islands around the city, including Randalls Island, Governors Island, Ellis Island, and Liberty Island, where the Statue of Liberty was completed in 1886.

Grinnell Library
2642 East Main St.
Wappingers Falls, NY 12590
845-297-3428

Long Island

Long Island stretches 120 miles to the east from New York City along the Atlantic Coast. Long Island is the largest island on the East Coast. More than two and a half million people live there. Many residents on the western part of the island work in New York City, so each weekday, hundreds of thousands of people **commute** by ferry or automobile to work.

To find out more about New York's regions, see the map on page 5.

NATURAL RESOURCES

Before the last **Ice Age,** Long Island was the eastern edge of a long, flat plain that ran from Pennsylvania's Allegheny Mountains to the Atlantic Ocean. A glacier

The pine barrens are pitch pine and oak tree forests with coastal ponds, red maple swamps, and other wetlands. They extend from central Long Island to the South Fork.

food from nearly any country in the world, including Ethiopia, Russia, Hungary, Jamaica, and Indonesia, to name a few.

ALL OVER NEW YORK

No matter where you travel in New York, you are certain to find a regional specialty. For example, some of the best wild **game** is prepared by roadside restaurants in the Catskills, while Binghamton residents rave about the *spiedie*, **marinated** chunks of barbecued beef eaten with Italian bread. The New York City bagel is a popular breakfast for New Yorkers, while the people of Long Island pride themselves on their fresh oysters. In addition, New York is also famous for its pizza, which comes in such unique varieties as taco pizza, pasta pizza, and chicken parmesan pizza.

At the foot of the Brooklyn Bridge, the Bridge Café is located in the city's oldest restaurant building, built in 1794.

Buffalo-style chicken wings were invented at the Anchor Bar, pictured on the left, in Buffalo in 1964.

New York's Culture

From Broadway shows to museums and art galleries, from concerts at Lincoln Center for the Performing Arts to jazz clubs, New York City is often thought of as the cultural capital of the country. In addition, New York state has a wide variety of cultural options.

BROADWAY

New York City's Broadway theater district is one of the most famous places in the world. Broadway got its name in the 1800s when it—with its central location—became the center of theater in New York City. The number of theaters on Broadway increased from about 20 in 1900

Times Square is popular around the holidays—more than 500,000 people come here to ring in the new year each year.

to an all-time high of 80 in 1925. During the record season of 1927–1928, 280 theaters were in operation. By 1980, only 40 theaters remained, and few of those were located on Broadway itself. Instead, the theaters were east or west of Broadway, between 41st and 53rd streets. However, since the 1980s, major new stages have drawn theater fans to the Times Square area of Broadway. Broadway's longest-running show is a musical called *Cats.* It ran from 1982 to 2001, with nearly 7,500 performances. In 2001, Broadway saw its highest attendance since 1959, with more than 11.9 million people attending shows. Broadway theaters also took in more than $666 million in 2001.

THE ARTS

New York is a paradise for art lovers. The state has offered a home, inspiration, and an audience to generations of artists. This is reflected in the busy galleries of the SoHo neighborhood and Madison Avenue in New York City, the dramatic sculpture gardens at Storm King Art Center in Mountainville, and the Metropolitan Museum of Art in New York City. Called the Met for short, it occupies four city blocks and is the largest art museum in the country.

The inside of the Guggenheim Museum is a six-floor spiral with galleries on each floor.

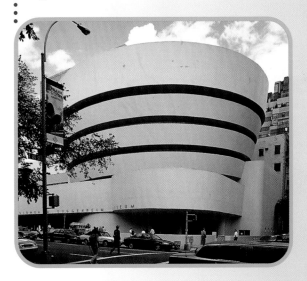

The columns at Storm King Art Center were originally intended to form part of the museum buildings but were instead placed outdoors as an individual display.

More than 300 million people have attended shows at Radio City since its opening in 1932.

THE MUSIC SCENE

Every type of music has been created in New York. Some of the most famous moments in music history have taken place in the state, including appearances of Elvis Presley and the Beatles on the *Ed Sullivan* television show, and the famous Woodstock music festival of 1969. More than 500,000 people came to Woodstock to hear such performers as the Grateful Dead, Santana, the Who, and Jimi Hendrix.

In New York City, the nightclubs of Harlem, Greenwich Village, and 52nd Street have long been important centers of influence in jazz and blues. The Apollo Theater is legendary for featuring African-American performers and amateur comedians, while the East Village clubs are hot spots of cutting-edge music. Rock fans can find a big-name band or performer, such as the Rolling Stones, every night in New York City, at large music halls such as Radio City Music Hall, the Beacon

Lincoln Center is the world's largest cultural complex with twelve different performing groups, including the New York City Ballet and the New York City Opera.

Theater, and Madison Square Garden. You can also find performances at smaller places, such as Irving Plaza and Acme Underground. Meanwhile, lovers of classical music, opera, and ballet can choose from many world-class venues, including Lincoln Center for the Performing Arts, City Center, Carnegie Hall, and the Brooklyn Academy of Music. At Lincoln Center, you can hear the New York Philharmonic Orchestra, which was founded in 1842. It is one of the oldest orchestras in the country.

CULTURE IN NEW YORK STATE

In 1960, New York became the first state to establish a Council for the Arts. As a result, 40 years later, every

The Saratoga Performing Arts Center is the summer home of the New York City Ballet and the Philadelphia Orchestra.

region is alive with **cultural** opportunities and entertainment. While Manhattan's Broadway theater district is the country's most famous, every part of New York has an exceptional venue for music and stage productions. The Saratoga Performing Arts Center is an open-air theater that presents everything from opera to ballet to rock concerts. In the state capital, the Palace Theatre is home to the Albany Symphony Orchestra. The Buffalo Philharmonic Orchestra performs in Kleinhans Music Hall. It is considered one of the five most **acoustically** perfect music halls in the world. Kleinhans Music Hall is a national historic landmark.

Legends and Lore

The **legends** and lore of the state—from Rip Van Winkle to UFOs—have helped to make New York famous.

MAKER OF MYTHS

The man who began the **myths** of New York was Washington Irving. He was considered by many to be the father of American literature. He lived nearly 200 years ago in the Hudson Valley. This was a time when long stretches of forest still separated farms and villages, and the mysterious Catskill Mountains stood in the distance.

Alligators in Manhattan

One of the most famous New York legends is the one that is most easily explained. For decades, city parents have been telling their terrified children about gigantic alligators roaming the sewers of Manhattan. The story got started in February of 1935, when the *New York Times* ran a story about a group of boys who discovered a reptile swimming in a sewer in Harlem. They managed to pull it out with a clothesline, but quickly realized their mistake when they were face-to-face with an angry alligator!

Irving was born in New York City, but he loved to listen to the wild stories told by the Dutch farmers who lived north of Manhattan. Irving's own writing contained characters and ideas borrowed from the tall tales the farmers told. Two stories in particular seem as fresh today as they did when he wrote them—"Rip Van Winkle" and "The Legend of Sleepy Hollow," both published in 1819.

Although Washington Irving never married or had children, he shared his home, Sunnyside, with his brother Ebenezer and Ebenezer's five daughters.

"RIP VAN WINKLE"

"Rip Van Winkle" is the story of a lazy man who ventures into the Catskills and ends up bowling and drinking with a band of dwarves. He falls into a deep sleep, and when he awakens, he finds that twenty years have passed. Rip returns home to find his wife has died, his daughter has married, and that he has slept through the American Revolution. This story lent an atmosphere of magic to the Catskills, which to some still seem far away and mysterious today.

"THE LEGEND OF SLEEPY HOLLOW"

"The Legend of Sleepy Hollow" is about a skinny schoolteacher named Ichabod Crane, who competes with the muscular Brom Bones for the love of Katrina Van Tassel, the daughter of a wealthy landowner. When Crane manages to gain an advantage in this contest, Bones disguises himself as a headless horseman and scares Crane out of town. This story was made into a famous cartoon in the 1940s and became a hit horror film in 2000.

HAUNTED NEW YORK

New York also has its share of haunted houses. The Merchant's House Museum, on East 4th Street, was built in 1830 by Seabury Tredwell, one of the richest men of his day. The house was occupied by members of the family until 1933, when Gertrude—the last surviving Tredwell—passed away. The house is furnished exactly as it would have been in the 1830s, which is probably

The Amityville Horror

New York's most famous haunting—and the one that has caused the most disagreement—occurred in Amityville, Long Island, in 1974. Ronald De Feo claimed that evil spirits inhabiting his house **possessed** him and made him murder his family. No one believed De Feo's story, and he was sent to jail. However, the next owners—George and Kathy Lutz—also claimed the house was overrun by evil spirits and moved out after a month. Shortly thereafter, they signed a book and movie deal and became quite wealthy from their misfortune. *The Amityville Horror* became a best-seller, and the film is considered a classic. Did the Lutzes really see ghosts, or were they looking to make a fortune from the day they moved in?

fine with Gertrude, whose ghostly presence makes regular appearances at the house. Witnesses of her ghost include museum workers, researchers, and even members of the press.

The strangest case of a haunting in New York occurred in the Hudson River village of Nyack, at the Ackley House. The state supreme court itself ruled the house was haunted! After paying $650,000 for the property in 1990, the buyers sued the seller because the seller failed to inform the buyers that the house had a long history of ghosts. The case went all the way to the state's supreme court, which ruled in the buyer's favor.

NEW YORK UFOS

Another odd event reported in the Hudson Valley is the appearance of unidentified

According to one owner of Ackley House, the ghosts occasionally leave gifts such as tiny silver tongs to toast a daughter's wedding or a golden baby ring to rattle in the birth of a child.

flying objects (UFOs) in an out-of-the-way area on the border of Ulster and Orange counties. The Pine Bush sightings were actually recorded by a camera crew from the television show *Sightings*, which was on location in the spring of 1993. Seven glowing objects were filmed hovering over the trees in an event that has never been fully explained.

New York's Sports

Since the beginning of professional team sports in the United States in the late 1800s, New York has been home to more than 200 different teams. Many of those teams have been based in and around New York City. One reason is that the country's largest city provides a large population in a concentrated area. As result, selling tickets to New York City sports events is rarely a problem.

GOLF AND BASKETBALL DEVELOP IN NEW YORK

The English game of golf arrived in the United States in the late 1800s. However, golf as an organized game is most often dated from the opening of the St. Andrews Golf Club in Yonkers in 1888. It is widely considered the first U.S. golf course. In 1894, the club held the first U.S. Open—a tournament where **amateurs** and professionals compete together.

Although the game of basketball was invented in Massachusetts, it started to gain national popularity in New York. The Buffalo Germans introduced the world to basketball at the 1901 fair called the Pan-American Exposition. In the 1920s, the New York Celtics—starring Nat Holman and Joe Lapchick—became the most talked–about team in the game. They played as part of the Eastern League. In the 1930s, the Harlem Renaissance, or Rens, made the game popular among African Americans. A New York sportswriter named Ned Irish set up the first major college basketball tournaments and turned Madison Square Garden into the center of the sport.

Name That Team

In the four major U.S. team sports alone—baseball, football, hockey, and basketball—New York has been home to more than 50 professional major league teams. These are just some of the teams associated with New York.

Baseball—Here Today
New York Yankees (1903–present)
New York Mets (1962–present)

Baseball—Change of Address
Brooklyn Dodgers (1890–1957; now in Los Angeles)
New York Giants (1883–1957; now in San Francisco)

Baseball—Long Gone
Brooklyn Gladiators (1890)
Brooklyn Hartfords (1877)
Brooklyn Tip-Tops (1914–1915)
Brooklyn Trolley Dodgers (1884–1889)
Brooklyn Wonders (1890)
Buffalo Blues (1914–1915)
Buffalo Bisons (1879–1885)
Buffalo Bisons (1890)
New York Giants (1890)
New York Metropolitans (1883–1887)
New York Mutuals (1871–1876)
Rochester Hop Bitters (1890)
Syracuse Stars (1879)
Troy Trojans (1879–1882)

Football—Here Today
Buffalo Bills (1960–present)

Football—Change of Address
New York Giants (1920–present; now play in New Jersey)

New York Jets (1960–present; now play in New Jersey)

Football—Long Gone
Brooklyn Dodgers (1930–1944)
Brooklyn Dodgers (1946–1948)
Brooklyn Horsemen (1926)
Brooklyn Lions (1926)
Buffalo All-Americans (1920–1929)
Buffalo Bisons (1946–1949)
Buffalo Indians (1940)
Buffalo Tigers (1941)
New York Americans (1941)
New York Bulldogs (1949–1951)
New York Yankees (1927–1928)
New York Yankees (1937)
New York Yankees (1946–1949)
Rochester Jeffersons (1920–1925)
Rochester Tigers (1936–1937)
Staten Island Stapletons (1929–1932)
Syracuse-Rochester Braves (1936)
Tonawanda Kardex (1921)

Hockey—Here Today
Buffalo Sabres (1970–present)
New York Islanders (1972–present)
New York Rangers (1926–present)

Hockey—Long Gone
New York Americans

(1925–1942)
New York Raiders/Golden Blades (1972–1974)

Basketball—Here Today
New York Knicks (1946–present)
New York Liberty (1997–present)

Basketball—Change of Address
New York Nets (1968–1976; now New Jersey Nets)
Rochester Royals (1945–1957; now Sacramento Kings)
Syracuse Nationals (1946–1963; now Philadelphia 76ers)

Basketball—Long Gone
Bronx Americans (1933)
Brooklyn Arcadians (1925–1926)
Brooklyn Celtics (1926)
Brooklyn Indians (1942–1944)
Brooklyn Visitations (1927–1939)
Buffalo Bisons (1925)
Buffalo Bisons (1946)
Kingston Colonials (1935–1940)
New York Americans (1943)
New York Celtics (1927–1930)
New York Gothams (1944–1946)
New York Hakoahs (1928–1929)
New York Jewels (1933–1943)
Rochester Centrals (1925–1931)
Syracuse All-Americans (1929)
Troy Haymakers (1938–1940)
Troy Celtics (1939–1941)

Note: Several independent professional basketball teams played in the 1920s, 1930s, and 1940s, including the New York Celtics, New York Rens, New York Yankees, Mohawk Redskins, and Syracuse Reds.

Horseplay is A-OK

For more than 175 years, New York has been the focus of summer horse racing. From late July to early September, Saratoga Springs is jammed with fans of thoroughbred racing. The Saratoga Race Course, built in 1864, is the oldest in the country. Each day more than 20,000 people attend the races. This number is roughly equal to the town's population the rest of the year!

The town of Goshen, in Orange County, is home to an even older track. It was built for **trotters** in the 1830s, and it is still used today. Nearby, in the town of Chester, is the grave of Hambletonian, history's most famous trotter. He sired, or fathered, more than 1,300 foals, and almost every trotter today is related to him in some way. The state's big harness-racing events are now held across the Hudson River, at Yonkers Raceway.

The two busiest horse-racing venues in New York are Aqueduct Racetrack, located in Queens, and Belmont Park, on Long Island. Belmont operates from May through October (except during the six weeks of Saratoga), while racing is held at Aqueduct in the colder months. Belmont is the site of the Belmont Stakes, the third leg of thoroughbred racing's famous Triple Crown.

BASEBALL

Baseball most likely began in New York. For many generations, **legend** said that the game was invented by Abner Doubleday in the village of Cooperstown in 1839. Historians have since found newspaper articles from the 1820s referring to games of "Base-Ball" in New York City. In the 1850s, the Atlantic Club of Brooklyn began paying a couple of its best players and charging the public admission to watch its games. This appears to be the beginning of professional baseball.

New York had also been an important center of African-American baseball teams. In 1885, Frank Thompson, the

headwaiter at the Argyle Hotel in Babylon, Long Island, got together some of the region's top baseball players to work at the hotel as waiters and play games for the entertainment of the guests. The team was so good it went on tour as the Cuban Giants, making it the first professional African-American sports team of any kind.

Not one member of the Cuban Giants was actually Cuban. They chose this name because of the belief that white people would not watch black athletes play.

Brooklyn was the site of another important event for baseball. In 1947, the Brooklyn Dodgers broke a long-standing racial barrier when they put Jackie Robinson in their lineup. Robinson was the first African American to play in Major League Baseball.

Another famous New York City team is the Yankees. The team has been playing in baseball's American League since 1903. The Yankees have had some of baseball's most famous players, including Babe Ruth, Lou Gehrig, Joe DiMaggio, Yogi Berra, Mickey Mantle, Reggie Jackson, and Derek Jeter. The team has won the World Series 26 times, including 4 of the last 7, in 1996 and 1998–2000.

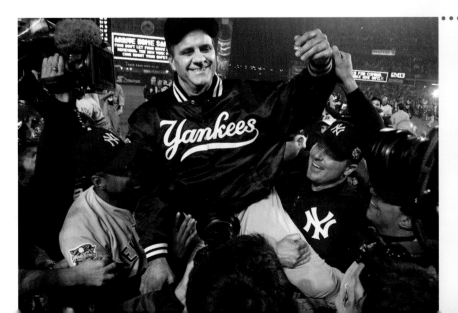

Two New York Yankees carry manager Joe Torre off the field after the Yankees won the 2000 World Series against their crosstown rival, the New York Mets.

Businesses and Products

New York has the second-largest state economy in the United States—trailing only California. Much of New York's economic might centers around New York City, but farming, manufacturing, and **exporting** are strong throughout the state.

NEW YORK CITY

New York City is considered the world's financial center. It is home to many companies, including more than 20 percent of the Fortune 500 companies—the 500 largest

New York City Businesses

Business	Fact
Finance	Banking headquarters for many of the nation's largest banks, including Citigroup—the world's largest bank
Publishing	One-third of all books published in the United States are published here
Retail	Midtown Manhattan is the country's largest retail center with more than 370,000 employees
Shipping	Port of New York-New Jersey is the nation's third busiest
Industry	Nation's third-largest manufacturing center with more than 17,000 plants and 430,000 workers

companies in the United States. One area that New York City has thrived in is advertising. In 1866, the world's first advertising agency, NW Ayer & Son, opened in New York City. The company is still doing business, along with more than 100 other advertising firms. The city has more advertising agencies than any other city in the country.

Much of the world's buying and selling activities flows through New York City every day. The best example of this is the New York Stock Exchange. Housed in a structure designed to look like a Roman temple, it is where **shares** of companies are bought, sold, and traded. From its opening in 1792, an entire district has grown up around it. It is the largest stock market in the world.

The New York Stock Exchange traces its roots to a meeting of 24 brokers that took place under a buttonwood tree on Wall Street in 1792.

New York is the **mass media** capital of the United States and the world. More publishing and broadcasting companies have their headquarters here than in any other place in the country. New York City is home to 60 radio and television networks, including the headquarters of ABC, NBC, and CBS. In addition, New York City's *Wall Street Journal,* a newspaper, leads the nation with a circulation of nearly two million. The *New York Times* is third in the nation with a circulation of more than one million.

The New York City subway contains 14 underwater tunnels and 68 bridges.

Transportation in and around New York City is an enormous business. More than 3.5 million people travel in and out of New York City each day. These commuters use all forms of transportation— boats, trains, buses, and cars. One of unique modes of transportation for New Yorkers is the 656-mile-long subway system, which opened in 1904. More than 1.3 billion riders take the subway every year. It is the busiest subway system in the country and the fifth busiest subway system in the world. New York City also has more than 4,300 buses. Bus drivers make more than 45,550 trips daily. Each rush hour, buses pick people up at more than 14,000 bus stops and carry 2.2 million people daily and 666 million annually. New York City bus drivers travel about 107 million miles every year—the equivalent of going to Mars and back. Commuters spend more than $200 million a year riding New York's buses and subways.

Another of New York City's most important businesses is the medical industry. It includes everything from making medicines to treating the sick to inventing new drugs and treatments. For example, Children's Hospital of New York Presbyterian ranks among the top five children's hospitals in the United States. Among the hospital's most notable accomplishments are the first hospital for infants in 1887 and the country's first successful heart transplant in a child in 1984.

NEW YORK STATE

Though most of New York's business is done in New York City, businesses thrive throughout the state. For

Medical Miracle

In the early years of the 1900s, the most dreaded enemy of New Yorkers was a disease called polio. It destroyed the muscles, leaving victims **paralyzed** or dead. Polio was caused by a virus, but no one was sure how people got it. There was no cure, and there was no way to prevent it. Polio seemed to afflict city children most often, and cases rose sharply during the summertime. Many parents simply bolted their doors, slammed their windows shut, and did not allow their children to go outside.

Jonas Salk, a student at New York University Medical School, decided to find a **vaccine** for polio. He learned all he could about viruses. After eight years of research, he had a vaccine ready to test in 1952—the same year a national outbreak occurred. In order to convince test subjects the vaccine was safe, Dr. Salk injected himself and his family.

Over the next few years, nearly two million schoolchildren tested the vaccine. By 1955, the vaccine was approved, and Dr. Salk was called a savior. He allowed the vaccine to be sold inexpensively to everyone. As a result, he made almost no money from his discovery.

example, New York farms rank in the top five nationally in the production of milk, apples, pears, cabbage, sweet corn, pumpkins, cucumbers, and maple syrup.

About 25 percent of New York is farmland, and there are about 37,500 farms in the state.

Corning's headquarters is nestled in the mountains of upstate New York.

New York is the country's third largest source of merchandise **export** sales, trailing only California and Texas. Four of the state's metropolitan areas—New York City, Rochester, Long Island, and Buffalo—are among the nation's top 50 areas for exporting goods. New York City exported more than all but six states in 1996, and both Rochester and Long Island accounted for more export sales than twenty states. These exports include electrical and electronic equipment, industrial equipment and computers, metal parts, and chemical products.

One important upstate industry is glass manufacturing. The town of Corning, located in the Finger Lakes region, was transformed into the glass-producing capital of the United States after the Civil War (1861–1865), when the Flint Glass Company moved there from Brooklyn. In the 1860s, the area's canal system made it ideal for shipping products all over the world.

As demand grew for different types of glass tubes and

Higher Learning

New York has an amazing variety of colleges and universities to choose from. The best known of New York's universities are Cornell and Columbia—both members of a respected group of universities called the Ivy League. Cornell, located in Ithaca, was founded in 1865. It has always offered a mix of traditional and nontraditional subjects and has never **discriminated** on the basis of race, sex, or religion. Columbia, located in upper Manhattan, was established in 1754 as King's College. It is most famous for its medical, law, and **journalism** schools.

A little more than 100 years ago, Columbia president Frederick Barnard founded Barnard College. Today, it ranks among the world's best women's colleges. Among New York City's other schools are New York University, St. John's, Fordham, and the Pratt Institute—all located within the five **boroughs.** Upstate are Hamilton, Hobart, Union, Syracuse, and Rochester. Another unique school is the U.S. Military Academy at West Point. It prepares the nation's men and women for careers as army officers.

lenses, the company expanded. Then, Thomas Edison invented the light bulb in 1879. Soon, Corning produced more than a million bulbs a day! Today, the company is focused on producing **fiber-optic** products for the computer industry. Also in Corning is the Steuben factory, where visitors can watch expert glass blowers at work.

Attractions and Landmarks

New York's attractions and landmarks contain such treasures as Niagara Falls, the Finger Lakes, and New York City's Central Park.

CENTRAL PARK

Central Park's trees, fields, footpaths, and ponds occupy 840 acres in the middle of New York City. The park was designed by Frederick Law Olmsted and completed over a twenty-year period in the mid-1800s. Although Central Park appears to be a completely natural setting, it is not. Olmsted and his partner, Calvert Vaux, carefully planned the position of every rock, bush, and tree. More than ten million cartloads of dirt were moved in the shaping of the park. Today, more than fifteen million people a year visit the park.

Central Park is home to the world's oldest zoo. It also has 21 playgrounds and an old-fashioned carousel.

New York State Parks

State Park

Coles Creek SP
Plattsburgh
Kring Point SP
Lake Champlain
Canoe Picnic Point SP
Lake Placid
Cedar Point SP
Burnham Point SP
Grass Point SP
Adirondack Mountains
Watertown
Ticonderoga
Westcott Beach SP

0   50 mi

Lake Ontario
Oswego
Delta Lake SP
Niagara Falls
Rome
Utica
Rochester
Chittenango Falls SP
Schenectady
Buffalo
Seneca Falls
Syracuse
Glimmerglass SP
Lake Erie
Cooperstown
Albany
Dansville
Max V. Shaul SP
Ithaca
Hudson River Island SP
Hudson
Binghamton
Catskill Mountains
Kingston
Poughkeepsie
Allegany SP
Appalachian National Scenic Trail
Harriman SP

Five Boroughs

Roberto Clemente SP
Rutherford
Ft. Lee
Bronx
North Bergen
Riverbank SP
Hudson River
Kearny
Union City
Hoboken
Manhattan
Newark
Queens
Empire-Fulton Ferry SP
Jersey City
Elizabeth
N.J.
N.Y.
Linden
Brooklyn
Staten Island
Bayswater SP
Clay Pit Ponds SP
Atlantic Ocean

Montauk
Bay Shore
Fire Island National Seashore
New York City

Long Island

Gov. Alfred E. Smith/ Sunken Meadow SP
Orient Beach SP
Bayard Cutting SP
Long Island Sound
Montauk
Belmont Lake SP
Bethpage SP
Wildwood SP
Sag Harbor SP
Caumsett SP
Planting Fields Arboretum SP
Brookhaven SP
Caleb Smith SP
Napeague SP
Connetquot River SP
Hither Hills SP
New York City
Heckscher SP
Montauk Downs SP
Sanctuary SP
Valley Stream SP
Captree SP
Camp Hero SP
Bay Shore
Montauk Point SP
Gilgo SP
Robert Moses SP
Hempstead Lake SP
Jones Beach SP
Atlantic Ocean

NATURAL WONDERS

Traveling north from New York City, the Adirondack Mountains are some of the largest peaks in the northeast and part of the 2.6-million-acre Adirondack Forest Preserve. The Adirondacks have two peaks of more than 5,000 feet.

East of the mountains are Lake George and Lake Champlain, which make up the water route that connects the

New York has a total of 168 state parks. The most popular ones are shown on this map.

There are actually 1,864 islands that make up the Thousand Islands region. To become an official part of the count, an island must be above water 365 days a year, and it must support two living trees.

St. Lawrence River with the Hudson River. These long, deep bodies of water attract hundreds of thousands of water sports participants every year.

To the north and west of the Adirondacks are the Thousand Islands, located in the St. Lawrence River between Cape Vincent and Alexandria Bay. There are actually over 1,800 islands in this region. South and west of the mountains are New York's Finger Lakes—ten long, narrow bodies of water cut by glaciers that resemble the fingers on two hands. The lakes create a moist and **fertile microclimate** that is ideal for fruit growing. New York's major **vineyards** are located here.

At the western edge of the state is Niagara Falls, one of the most breathtaking spots in the world. It is actually a set of three falls—American Falls and Bridal Veil Falls on the U.S. side of the Niagara River, and Horseshoe Falls on the Canadian side. The water rushing over the tow-

Adirondack State Park, with over six million acres of land, is the size of the state of Vermont.

ering 1,000-foot rocks moves from Lake Erie to Lake Ontario. Each year, more than twelve million people visit Niagara Falls. It also has the fastest water flow rate of any waterfall in the world. More than 150,000 gallons of water flow over the falls every second.

Only in New York

The list of unique and unusual places in New York includes many other landmarks and attractions. Among the most popular are the National Baseball Hall of Fame and Museum in Cooperstown, the Franklin D. Roosevelt National Historic Site in Hyde Park, and the mineral baths at Saratoga Springs.

Among the most unusual places are the 300-year-old sunken forest on Long Island; the 23-acre Riverbank Park, which is built atop a Harlem sewage treatment plant; and the Herkimer Diamond Mine. There is also Binghamton's six antique carousels; the birthplace of Jell-O in Le Roy; the Goodrich Motel in Avoca, where guests sleep in train cabooses; and the Muskie Hall of Fame in Clayton. It is probably the only hall of fame devoted to a fish.

A replica of the 69-pound, 15-ounce world-record muskie caught in Lake Ontario in 1957 is on display at the Muskie Hall of Fame.

Buildings and Structures

Throughout New York, bridges, buildings, tunnels, and other human-made marvels dot the state.

SKYSCRAPER CITY

In New York City, tall buildings are how people recognize the Manhattan skyline. One of the most recognizable is the Empire State Building, located on 34th street and 5th Avenue. Completed in 1931, it took only 14 months to build, and at more than 100 stories was the tallest building in the world until the 1970s. Millions of people have viewed the city from its observation decks on the 86th and 102nd floors.

Eight blocks north and three blocks east is the Chrysler Building. Built in 1930 as a monument to the American automobile industry, it was the world's tallest building until the Empire State was completed. It features a gleaming, stainless steel **spire** and **gargoyles** that look like car hood ornaments. In

The Empire State Building contains 6,500 windows and 73 elevators.

Completed in 1934, 30 Rockefeller Center became the RCA headquarters. General Electric's initials now brighten the rooftop of the home of NBC Studios.

some places, the building's brickwork resembles wheels and hubcaps.

For many years before either of these skyscrapers went up, the world's tallest building was located a couple of miles downtown. The Woolworth Building, finished in 1913, has gleamming walls and green copper roofs.

Between Fifth Avenue and Avenue of the Americas is a group of nineteen buildings called Rockefeller Center. Every part of the complex offers a different treat for the eyes, and at Christmas time, an enormous tree is set up next to the famous ice rink. The yearly lighting of the tree has become a major New York City event.

Across the street from Rockefeller Center is New York City's most famous church, St. Patrick's Cathedral. It is one of many impressive religious

The Chrysler Building is recognized as New York City's greatest display of art deco, a decorative style of building design that features sharp zigzag surface forms and ornaments.

Roman Catholic leaders of New York are buried under the high altar at St. Patrick's Cathedral.

buildings in the city, yet it is far from the biggest. That honor belongs to the Cathedral of St. John the Divine, on 110th Street. It is the largest cathedral of its kind in the world. Paris's famous Notre Dame Cathedral could easily fit inside.

HOUSING

New York City's 7.5 million people live in a variety of housing, from townhomes to apartments. Most New Yorkers—about 65 percent—live in apartments and about 70 percent rent their homes rather than own them. About half the housing in the city was built before 1940. Some of New York's most unique homes are in Brooklyn. Two of its oldest neighborhoods—Brooklyn Heights and Cobble Hill—have more than 1,000 houses that are 100 years old or more.

Colorful brownstone homes line the streets of Brooklyn Heights.

BRIDGES

Among other architectural marvels in New York City are its many bridges. The most impressive is the Brooklyn Bridge. Opened in 1883, it spans the East River and connects Manhattan with Brooklyn. It was the world's first steel **suspension bridge.** Another bridge, called the Verrazano Narrows, was built in 1964. Spanning 4,260 feet, it has the longest bridge span in the United States, and it is the second-longest suspension bridge in the world.

In 1884, circus owner P. T. Barnum demonstrated the safety of the Brooklyn Bridge by parading across it with a herd of 21 elephants.

THE STATUE OF LIBERTY

Visible from the Brooklyn Bridge is New York's most famous architectural landmark, the Statue of Liberty. Originally called "Liberty Enlightening the World," the statue is 151 feet high and weighs more than 200 tons. The skin is copper, while the support structure is made of steel. The sculpture was designed by French sculptor Frederic

Auguste Bartholdi. The statue was a gift of friendship from the people of France to the United States to celebrate the 100th anniversary of American independence.

Work on the statue began in France in 1875 and was completed in 1885. The pieces of the statue were assembled on the star-shaped wooden base on Ellis Island. The Statue of Liberty was the first thing millions of **immigrants** saw as they entered New York Harbor by boat to start a new life in the United States.

Statue of Liberty Facts

- Its massive right arm was put on temporary display in Manhattan's Madison Square Park in 1876—and stayed there for seven years until enough money could be raised to complete the statue's base.
- The statue crossed the Atlantic Ocean by ship in a total of 214 crates.
- The seven spikes on the statue's crown represent the seven continents of the world.
- There are 354 steps from the statue's base to its crown.

Map of New York

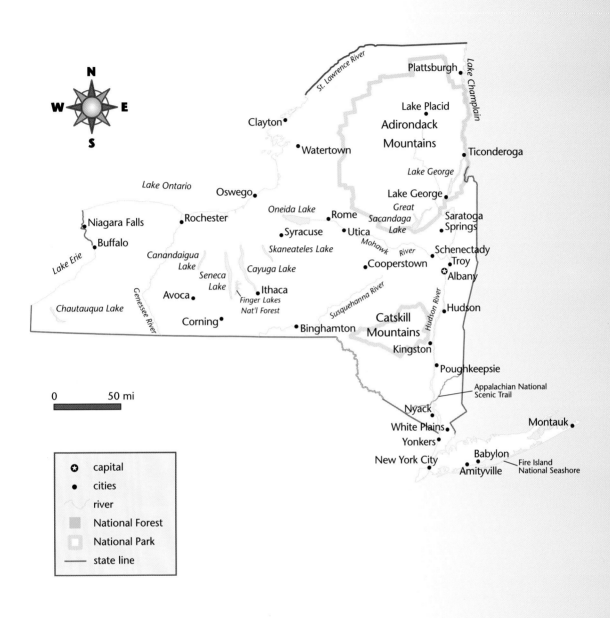

N
W E
S

St. Lawrence River

Plattsburgh

Lake Champlain

Clayton

Lake Placid

Adirondack
Mountains

Watertown

Ticonderoga

Lake George

Lake Ontario

Oswego

Lake George

Great
Sacandaga
Lake

Saratoga
Springs

Oneida Lake

Rome

Niagara Falls

Rochester

Syracuse

Utica

Mohawk

River

Schenectady

Buffalo

Skaneateles Lake

Cooperstown

Troy

Albany

Lake Erie

Canandaigua
Lake

Cayuga Lake

Seneca
Lake

Hudson River

Avoca

Ithaca

Finger Lakes
Nat'l Forest

Susquehanna River

Catskill
Mountains

Hudson

Chautauqua Lake

Genesee River

Corning

Binghamton

Kingston

Poughkeepsie

0   50 mi

Appalachian National
Scenic Trail

Nyack

Montauk

White Plains

Yonkers

Babylon

New York City

Fire Island
National Seashore

Amityville

⊗ capital
• cities
   river
▣ National Forest
▢ National Park
— state line

CANADA

Maine

Vermont

New
Hampshire

New York

Massachusetts

Rhode Island
Connecticut

Ohio

Pennsylvania

New
Jersey

Atlantic
Ocean

Glossary

acoustic related to the hearing of sound

amateur person who takes part in sports for pleasure and not pay

appeal asking a court to decide on a judgement made by a lower court

assembly lawmaking body

borough one of the five political divisions of New York City; a self-governing town or village in some states

budget plan for using money

bust sculpture of the upper part of a human being that includes the head and neck

capitol building in which the legislature meets

constitution basic beliefs and laws of a nation or state in which the powers and duties of government are established and certain rights are guaranteed to the people

cultural ideas, skills, arts, and a way of life of a certain people at a certain time

discriminate treat people unfairly based on their differences from others

ethnic belonging to a group with a particular culture

executive branch part of the government that carries out the laws

export sell goods to other countries; a good sold to other countries

extinct no longer living

fertile bearing crops or vegetation in abundance

fiber-optic thin, transparent fibers of glass or plastic that allow light to pass throughout their length

game animal hunted for food or sport

gargoyle waterspout in the form of a strange or frightening human or animal figure sticking out at the roof or eaves of a building

governor person elected to be the head of a state of the United States; the governor is the head of the executive branch of a state government

immigrant one who moves to another country to settle

journalism business of collecting and editing news for newspapers, magazines, and television

judicial branch part of the government that decides how laws can be applied

legend old story that is widely believed but cannot be proved to be true

legislative branch part of the government that makes and changes laws

liberty cap a small, snug cap that was worn by freed slaves in ancient Rome. Liberty caps were worn in the United States in the 1700s as a sign of freedom.

lore common knowledge or beliefs

marinate to soak vegetable or meat in a sauce

mass media the ways of communicating to many people, such as the newspaper, radio, television, and the Internet

microclimate a uniform climate in an unusually small area or habitat

motto a brief statement used to express an important idea or belief

myth legend that tells about a being with more than human powers or an event which cannot be explained or that explains a religious belief or practice

paralyzed unable to move or feel parts of the body

possessed to be controlled by

senate upper and smaller branch of a legislature in a country or state

shares equal parts into which the value of a company is divided. When people buy shares, they own part of the company.

spire pointed roof, especially of a tower

stock exchange place where stock shares are bought and sold

suspension bridge a type of bridge that hangs from strong cables

trotter horse trained for harness racing

vaccine material used to protect against disease

vineyard a place where grapevines can be grown

Western Hemisphere half of the earth that has North and South America and the surrounding waters

More Books to Read

Heinrichs, Ann. *New York*. Minneapolis: Compass Point Books, 2002.

Kent, Deborah. *New York City*. Danbury, Conn.: Scholastic Library Publishing, 2000.

Munro, Roxie. *The Inside-Outside Book of New York City*. New York City: SeaStar Books, 2001.

Shapiro, Ellen R. *New York City with Kids*. New York City: Crown Publishing Group, 2003.

Index

About the Author

Mark Stewart was born and raised in New York City and now lives across the water in New Jersey, where his office overlooks the metropolitan skyline. A graduate of Duke University with a degree in history, Stewart has authored more than 100 nonfiction titles for the school and library market. He and his wife Sarah have two daughters, Mariah and Rachel.